MW01488519

The Other Side
By C.M. Healy
Copyright 2015 C.M. Healy
Printed by CreateSpace
ISBN 978-1539022138

CreateSpace, License Notes

All rights reserved. No part of this publication may be reproduced, stored in a retrieval system, or transmitted, in any form or by any means, electronic, mechanical, photo-copying, recording or otherwise, without the prior permission of the publisher and copyright owner. Book is available for ebook purchase at any ebook retailer.

To Arbor Creek MS,
Explore the other side.

Table of Contents

The Other Side

What are we like on the other side?
Are we round like a ball?
Would we stand ten feet tall?
Do we still have two eyes and ten toes?
Are we stinky and mean?
Unkempt and unclean?
Never washing ourselves or our clothes?

How would we dress on the other side?
Put our gloves on our feet?
Wear thick coats in the heat?
Maybe turn all our pants inside out?
Put our hats on our bums?
Wear all plaid just for fun?
Maybe dress in a suit made of trout?

What would we eat on the other side?
Fuzzy cheese with green mold?
Soggy pizza that's old?
Wash it down with milk curdled with lumps?
Stale crackers and chips?
Rotten French onion dips?
For dessert chocolate mousse with hair clumps?

How would we talk on the other side?
Would our language be strange?
All our words rearranged?
Sounding weird to our family and friends?
We could whistle or blink it?
Perhaps only think it?
Speaking solely with thoughts that we send?

So I can't really say,
what we're like day to day
on the other side of this great mirror.
They might have way more fun,
live to be one-oh-one,
but I think I'm glad I'm over here.

The Other Side

What are we like on the other side?
Are we thin as a rail?
Maybe short like a snail?
Do we have colored eyes and a nose?
Are we pretty and kind?
Nice and neat like we mind?
Bathing daily and wearing clean clothes?

How would we dress on the other side?
Put our shirts on our tops?
On our feet wear flip-flops?
Maybe put on a high-heel or two?
Wear our hats on our heads?
Get dress up in silk threads?
Wear a fitted suit dyed royal blue?

What would we eat on the other side?
Fresh cut salad with cheese?
T-bone steak if you please?
Wash it down with a bottle of wine?
Caviar, escargot?
Spread on bread of rye dough?
For dessert a smooth sherbet of lime?

How would we talk on the other side?
Act out words like a mime?
Use our hands to make signs?
A world silent, where no one would speak?
Or use our lips and our tongues?
To send sounds to someone?
And then whisper when secrets to leak?

So I can't really say,
what we're like day to day
on the other side of this great mirror.
they might have way more fun,
live to be one-oh-one,
but I think I'm glad I'm over here.

4

The Mission Part I

It was all too easy for a pro like me
A present wrapped nicely under the tree
Just out in plain view like a sitting duck
I call it skill, but some call it luck
There were two different boxes, but exactly the same
One labeled for my brother, the other my name
See I knew the contents of my brother's gift
A mechanical dog that would bark and would sit
It was the mystery of mine that made me insane
And was driving me slowly down criminal lane
I needed a plot to unwrap my gift now
But the question was when and the question was how
I knew when time came I'd have to be quick
I had to be careful which one I would pick
So hours in advance I set mine aside
To know just where my gift would reside
Just some nonchalant looks, a shake here and there
Disguised my true intent of secretly where
I placed my gift, in a camouflaged spot,
Would the parents suspect? Oh, no I think not.
Yes, all to do now was to sit back and wait…

To my surprise it is right around eight
The ladies are leaving to shop around town
They have no idea what's about to go down
The greatest heist in all Christmas history
That will finally solve the puzzling gift mystery
The dads will be there, but please, are you kidding
They'll be talking all night, at the table be sitting
With all the girls gone and the dads unaware
I quickly decide now's the time for my snare.

Slowly I descend down the stairs

               not

                 a

                  peep

And into the living room I cautiously creep

As my hand goes out blindly to locate my gift

I keep an eye on where all the dads sit

They have no idea, they just all go on talking

While demise is coming for the present I'm stalking

A quick check to make sure that it is the one

Then off up the stairs I take off in a run

No one has heard me, it goes down like the plan

I can hardly believe it, I think "I'm the man!"

I sit down on the floor and begin to tear paper

To see my reward of the Great Christmas Caper

A new toy to play with or some sneakers to jog

What could it be? It's, it's A MECHANICAL DOG!??

How… I… what?

Oh well, there's always next year.

Thirsty

Give gifts to your mom
Like scarves of fine silk
So she'll give you treats
Like cookies and

Gummy

My friend's life is pretty crummy,
And it really isn't funny
When I tell you all his strange
predicament.
He's lost every single tooth,
he simply said, "They all came looth."
So his days of chewing food have
came and went.

He can't eat his favorite things.
No more flavored chicken wings.
No more need for moist towelettes
or fancy bibs.
No more Hawaiian roasted hogs,
or fully loaded chili dogs,
no more Ray's delicious barbeque
smoked ribs.

He's been out a couple times,
with his toothy friends to dine,
but watching simply made it worse in
many ways.
They ate steak and fresh piranha,
char-grilled burgers and iguana;
it made him long for his old chomping,
grinding days.

He can't have lamb or fried pork chops,
or tender veal with sauce on top,
even shepherd's pie is hard for him
to chew.
His cherished meal was slow-cooked brisket.
Pulled or sliced he sure does miss it.
Such cuisine he can enjoy is far and few.

You see there just aren't many foods
that will brighten up his mood;
slurping soup and cream-of-corn just
don't feel right.
Mashed potatoes are too bland,
he despises stuff in cans
and baby food can't satisfy his appetite.

He can sometimes gnaw on fish,
because it's the only dish
he can gum, but still it takes him
most the day.
His friends all bought him bendy straws
and a blender for his cause,
but it doesn't taste the same when
meat's pureed.

So I think you must admit
that my story's quite legit,
and a life without your teeth would
be just crummy.
But imagine if you will,
the tale I've told gets much worse still,

8

because my friend's a T-Rex
everyone calls Gummy.

How Does the Grass Grow Green?

How does the grass grow green?

Is it because it awakes to the clear water drops of morning dew?
Or perhaps because it flourishes with the sun's yellow beams under a sky of blue?
Maybe it's because it slumbers with the black blanket of night
And the stars twinkling bright with the light of the pale moon white
I know it's eaten by a brown cow,
                              so now,
                                          can anyone tell me how

the grass grows green?

Cryin' Lion

I once knew a lion who couldn't stop cryin'
'cause somebody stepped on his tail.

See try as he must he still whimpered and fussed
and chewed all of but one of his nails.

It's possible maybe he's just a big baby,
who cries all the time but I think,

the reason he wails is his beautiful tail
is now ruined by an imperfect kink.

How High Can a Balloon Fly?

How high can a balloon fly
when it soars into the sky?

Can it soar straight to the moon?
I hope it comes back sometime soon.
You see it was my favorite balloon,
I lost it sometime around noon.

A strong breeze came and took it away.
Like I said, around noon today.
Came and took it right from my hand.
It's something I really don't understand.

But my balloon loves me like I love it
so that's why I wait here and I sit,
in the rain just getting wetter
waiting for my balloon's first letter.

Telling of all the places it's seeing,
flying high above cities all gleaming,
going as far as Timbuktu –
My balloon might pass right over you.

It's red, big and round, and oh, yeah, there's a string
Tied tight 'round the bottom to hold on to the thing.
So if you should happen to see my balloon,
please tell it to come back home to me soon.

You see it's my friend, and I love it most dear
that's why I am waiting and sitting right here
in the rain by the mailbox just getting wetter
hoping my balloon comes home. . .

. . .or at least sends me a letter.

The Baker

Way up high, and far beyond the normal reach of clouds
There lives a man with silver hair where no one is allowed
He's all alone ,but doesn't mind because he loves his job
It keeps him very entertained, a chef of sorts, but odd
He travels 'round the world you see, it's not a local thing
From Scotland Yard to Katmandu, his works have all been seen
He searches for ingredients and stuffs them in a sack
A burlap bag with many patches slung across his back
To his shop he saunters back to start his works of art
He thinks today he'll start off with one favorite to his heart
He's been, at times, compared by some to workers of great skill
Mixing, kneading, pulling like an artist, if you will
He starts by stirring special mixes in a giant pot
And stokes the fire while he goes to make sure that it's hot
Once his great concoction's done, there still remain some lumps
But that's the trick to his creations, making them with bumps
He pulls the mixture from the pot and pounds and kneads away
Stretching, rolling, molding like a dough in many ways
He puts it gently on the pan and slides it in the oven
Three-fifty for an hour is just the right amount of lovin'
The timer dings, the baking's done, to him it's sheer perfection
His favorite since he started, it's a bunny shaped confection

14

Carefully he picks it up and takes it to the door
With deepest breath, he blows it out across the Eastern shore
And far below the people on the beach see something funny
They look up in the sky and see a cloud shaped like a bunny

The Juggler

Gather 'round, gather 'round all you people in town
For a feat your eyes may not believe
Come near or come far from wherever you are
I promise you won't want to leave.
I have many names, but it's me all the same
And I'm known across all of the lands
For I am the Stunning Most Daring Most Cunning
Majestical Bim Zala Zands.
I have seen many faces and been many places
To learn everything there is to know.
From monks who are Turkish and clowns in the circus
To give you the greatest of shows.
I'm a juggler you see, and the best that will be
All my life I have practiced and trained
For my name to be up on a sign and lit up
Bringing fortune and glory and fame.
I start it off small with just one, single ball
But then quickly add two or three more
And then right after that I toss in a top hat
And an apple I eat to the core.
Next up is the fire, it's what you desire
Some torches and maybe some rings
Imagine it now, all you're thinking is "How
Can he possibly add one more thing?"

Add three breakable plates, and sharp ice skating skates
And a gentleman's old tattered shoe,
A small fish in a glass and a pig made of brass
Sure, let's toss in a bowling ball too.
A black cat and a frog, I will juggle a dog
If it pleases and dazzles your eyes,
A fried chicken or duck, and a tiny toy truck
What's up next you can only surmise.
A red pair of wax lips, an old bag of stale chips
And a petrified slice of fruit cake,
A set of chess pieces, two fake Mona Lisas
And just for a challenge, a rake.
A pink twirling baton, three chainsaws that are on
To ensure it endangers my life,
Behind back, under leg, add a half dozen eggs
As I throw in a large hunting knife.
Ooh, let's add in some fruit and a marching band flute
Envision it all going higher
It's incredible yes? Just admit you're impressed...

'Scuse me sir...did you call me a liar?

You think I'm all talk and I can't walk the walk
Well the show is about to begin.
But please do understand, that once things are in hand
I can't stop, you won't see it again.
Now it's time for the fun, so stand back everyone
And allow me to gather my gear,
All the items I have in my black duffle bag
I sat it down right over ....

17

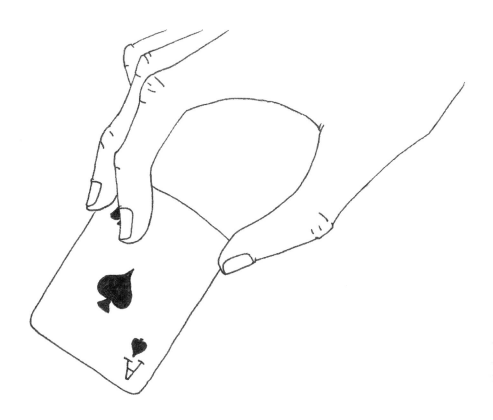

Huh...well that's strange. I could've sworn I....set it down.......right over....
Hmmm.
Would anyone be interested in a card trick?

Spare Some

While walking down the street one day
I came 'cross something odd
A clown was on the corner
But not quite doing his job.
Instead of making people smile
Or handing out some laughs
He panicked on the sidewalk
With balloons shaped like giraffes.
"Excuse me folks could someone help
A clown down on his luck?
It isn't what you're thinking
I don't need your change or buck
I seem to have run out
Of my supply of 'ha's' and 'hee's,'
So see it isn't much to ask,
Could someone help me please?
Uh, pardon ma'am, but could ya spare
A small snicker or two?
Oh, thank you ma'am, you're such a saint
I'll say God bless you too.
I've got a children's birthday gig
At three o'clock today
Hey mister, lend me out a snort
C'mon what do ya say?
Why thank ya kindly sir for all your snorts
And then some giggles
Now all the kids will laugh
When I begin to dance and wiggle.
Excuse me sir, would you might have
A spare grin or a smirk
A disapproving frown?
That doesn't really help me (Jerk)."

I couldn't offer much but put
Some chuckles in his cup
He thanked me, tossed them in his bag
And promptly tied it up.

I never saw the clown again
I figure he's all right,
I'm sure he's making people smile
Whoever's in his sight.
But if you see a desperate man
That's dressed up like a clown
Who's standing on a corner
In the middle of downtown
Please take some time to give a laugh
To help him on his way
You might just get one back sometime
To brighten up your day.

The Cliff

This is the year.
This is the year that I conquer my fear
And jump off of that ridiculous cliff
It's incredibly high (I heard once a kid died)
But not really it's all just a myth
It hangs over a lake that's laid out like a snake
There's a rope swing that hangs down below
As some people leap out they might scream or they shout
"Here I come," or perhaps "Tally ho!"
I've gone up many times but I simply can't find
Enough courage to run off and jump
So this year I swear, don't look down don't you dare
And get over my mental block hump
There's a path you can climb,
and it twists,
turns and w
i
n
d
s
To the top of the monstrous beast
It looks much higher then,
makes your hair stand on end
It's a daunting view to say the least
Cross your arms, point your toes,
these things everyone knows
It's the one thing that runs thru my mind
I've been up here forever,
it's now or it's never
I search, and my courage I find

I don't dare take a peep, but prepare for my leap
    I stand back and get ready to run
Deep breath in, deep breath out, I get rid of my doubt
    Left right left...and the deed has been done
The cool air rushes by, it feels like I can fly
    Almost if I was in a daydream
But the water comes fast and I make a big splash
    Cutting short my best girly-man scream
        I pop up, I'm okay, it's a momentous day
        I'm not scared of the cliff anymore
My grin stretches so wide,
    I swim off with great pride
        And stand up on the lake's rocky shore
People cheer and applaud, giving whistles and nods
    My accomplishment's hardly minute
Then I feel a small breeze coming up from my knees
    I seem to have lost my

            swim suit.

The Transformation

My mom used to say "Close your mouth when you chew"
Because apparently that's just something you don't do

"Stop picking your nose!" she'd yell at me
Worried that some of her friends might see

Occasionally the frequent "Stop hitting your brother"
Is just one of the phrases that came from my mother

At dinner I'd hear "Quit playing with your food!"
It seems to me she was always in a bad mood

To help me "build character" I push mowed the lawn
And always to cover my mouth when I yawn

"Put some socks on" she'd say "or you'll catch a cold"
It didn't take long for that phrase to get old

"If all your friends jumped, would you jump off too?"
Sometimes I'd say "Yes." just to see what she'd do

When I would go out "Put on clean underwear,"
In case of an accident, I'm so glad she cares

Time has passed now, I'm older and grown
I married a girl and have kids of my own

Most people think they're just bundles of fun
But I've something to say of my daughter and son

They've tested my patience, my lovely wife's too
When they know that they shouldn't but still instead do

I've tried to be calm, using logic and reason
I swear though, at times, they're like little demons

Questioning everything that you might say
Poking and prodding us both every day

You try hard to explain of why they cannot
But they don't understand and that happens a lot

My mom knew it would come, that I'd have my day
When I'd run out of cool and have nothing to say

It's the most common phrase that all parents will use
The bombardment of back-talk just blows out their fuse

You've had it to here, the last straw is broken
You can't take it back, the phrase has been spoken

The words just come out, not a cuss, not a lie
Something far worse that I think I might die

I've turned into my mom, when or how I don't know
But I hear myself saying "Because I said so!"

Memory Boxes

For every new thing that I learn how to do
(Like today I relearned how to tie my own shoe)
I forget something else that I've learned in the past
Like is number one first or is number one last
I think that these things must slip right out my ear
Because every so often it's quite hard to hear
The new things must push the old things right out
Out my head, through my ear I have not a doubt
You see in my head there is limited space
If I meet someone new, I forget an old face
So I figured a way to keep track of old things
I'd store them in boxes tied up with gold strings
Right under my ear the boxes would go
To catch all those things that I used to know
Out with the old as the new things come in
Fresh places take over the places I've been
Filled to the brim, tied with long strings of gold
Let me tell you some things that these old boxes hold,

Things like . . .
Addresses and names, instructions to games
To open umbrellas whenever it rains
Like how to skip rope, to pout when I mope
I think that there's also some names of the Pope
How to color and scribble, to munch or to nibble
And especially skills of my basketball dribble
Do my pants go on first, do I drink when I thirst
Which smells are okay and which ones are the worst
How to cough, how to sneeze, how to climb up tall trees
Most importantly when to say "Thank you" and "Please"
Two plus two equals four, for girls open the door
I've got all kinds of stuff would you like to hear more?
How to scream when I'm scared, how to shampoo my hair
To play dead when attacked by a big grizzly bear
To chew first then swallow, the earth is not hollow
Sometimes you can lead and sometimes you should follow
Blowing up a balloon, eating lunch around noon
That a cat and a mouse are my favorite cartoon
To laugh at a clown, how to smile and frown
That to stand on my head turns my world upside down.

So I knew many things that I've now forgot
Sad but it's true, it happens a lot
But recall if you will, I can save my old thoughts
When a new thing comes in, an old falls in a box
Now you'd think that I'd store these things somewhere up safe
But no one will steal them of this I have faith
They hold nothing valued or even much worth
Unless you want thoughts from my long ago birth
And I put all my boxes wherever they'll fit
Some just lie in a chair so please watch where you sit
I put boxes right here and put boxes right there
There's even a box 'neath my clean underwear
I put boxes up high, I put boxes down low
There's some boxes I've lost so those things I don't know
It's crazy to think how life might or could be
If I forgot when to sleep or forgot how to pee
Oh my word what's the time are you sure that is right
I've been talking all day, it has now become night
Well I'm running late now, but for what I don't know
Still I must ask a question before we both go
Your name once again as we part and say bye
(slip. . . whoops. Oh bother.)
Can you tell me now friend, I forgot, who am I?

Who Does a Superhero Talk to at the End of the Day?

When all is said and done
And the good guys have just won
Who do they go to talk to?
Their mother their father
Some don't even bother
And just sit with nothing to do.

Do they drive around town
Or go home and lie down
With thoughts of the people they've saved?
The strong and the weak,
The bold and the meek
"All in a days work!" they would say.

With their hands bound up tight
To the villain's delight
He reveals his great dastardly plot.
Then the hero breaks free
"You're coming with me!"
And the good guys come out on the top.

I'm sure they get tired
Of the bad guy who's wired
And wants to take over the earth.
But I bet it feels good
(And I would if I could)
Save the one life for what it is worth.

Is there some sort of gang
Where they just sit and hang
And dwell on the life they had lost?
I know that they care
And give up they don't dare
But keep fighting whatever the cost.

When they're running around
Or go flying downtown
It cannot be very easy,
To risk their own life
And go through all the strife
To save someone like you or me.

So this that I say
The price that they pay
Is worth more that we can all give.
So lend them an ear
Whenever they're near
They fight on, so we all can live.

Tony Two-Toes

So my good friend Tony Two-Toes only gots two toes, that's how he got his name
He used to have ten, now he's only gots two, and he's never been the same.

The problem see is ol' Tony won't put his feet inside any type of shoe
He swears his feet are claustrophobic and there's really not much he can do
So he walks around barefoot, most all the time, it's toughened up his skin
The bottoms of his feet do fine, but his toes just never seem to win.

He lost the first two when he was only ten while visiting a farm
He went straight for the chickens, his first mistake, when he walked into the barn
A big fat hen came cluckin' in and eyed his pinky toes
She must have thought they were big fat worms 'cause she gobbled 'em down just so.

The next one came on a dare, he had just turned thirteen and a half
The challenge was to stand barefoot out in the snow and he merely laughed
One by one his friends dropped out to seek the warm inside
When Tony won, a toe had turned black, yep it had surely died.

He was cleaning up his place one day, he had a lovely downtown loft
Well his vacuum hose got ahold of his big toe, and sucked the darn thing clean off.
Tony's wife convinced him to try shoes again and on that fateful day
His long boss toe took one scared look, simply screamed and ran away.

He lost the next two toes together on a family camping trip
He was chopping fire-wood up fine until he suddenly lost his grip
He grabbed his toes and hurried to the doctor to be fixed
But on arrival he realized instead he'd grabbed two stumpy sticks.

His most recent loss of toe number eight happened a few weeks ago
He surprised his daughter with front row seats to a big time magic show
Tony volunteered, of course, for the magician's final act
He made Tony's last three toes disappear, but could only get two back.

So my good friend Tony Two-toes, that's his story of how he lost eight toes
When or if he'll lose the last, let's hope not, but no one for sure knows
He'll probably…oh hang on a sec "Hey! Hey Tony! Look out for that mousetrap.
I said look out for that…"
SNAP!

So my good friend Tony One-Toe…

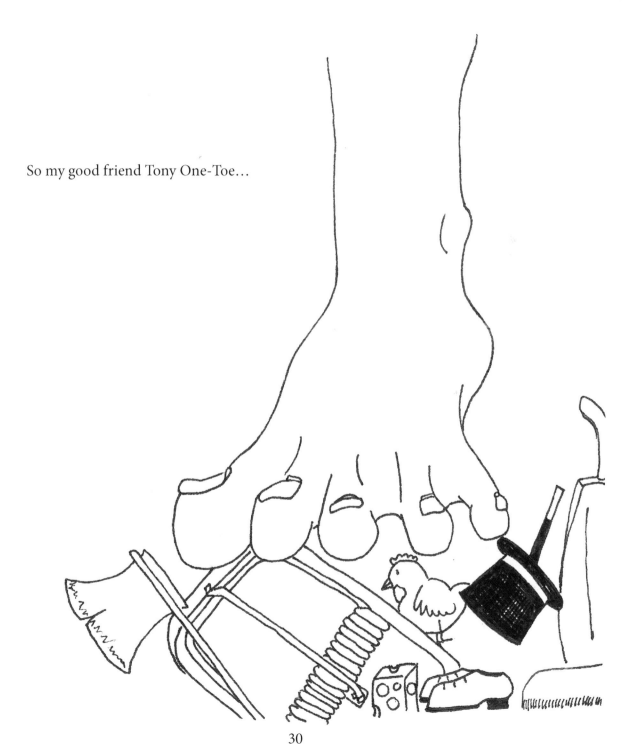

Missing Ingredient

Our parents all warned, "It is gonna be tough."
Yet we all came that day with all of our stuff.
Each one of us knew we could all pull it off,
Even Kyle showed up with his terrible cough.
I had to be there, I'm the leader of course,
Barry, Robin, and Mike (who was a little bit hoarse),
Stuart, Ryan and Sondra, and our dearest friend Nick,
Who turned up after all 'cause he wasn't that sick.
You'll never guess then who decided to show,
Our good friend from school Mr. Joe Eskimo.
There was Andy and Darla and Jimmy Labroze
(A kid down the street that nobody knows).
But he showed up today just to give us a hand
In building the world's best, gigantic snowman.
"I think that it's time we check everything off,"
Kyle managed to say through his terrible cough.
"We brought the red licorice," said Robin and Barry,
"It will make a great smile and make him look merry."

"We got the arms!" yelled out Stuart and Nick,
Then proceeded to show us a couple of sticks.
"I've got the grapes," cried out Jim, "for his toes!"
"There aren't any feet!" exclaimed Joe Eskimo.
"Oh really?" said Jimmy (who nobody knew),
"Then use this for a nose—a carrot I grew."
"Who's got the stuff for the buttons we like?"
"Right here's the coal," said our biggest friend Mike.
"I've got blue marbles," piped up Ryan, "for his eyes
But I'm sorry to say that they're not the same size."
Andy and Darla said, "We've got the broom."
I was beginning to think, Would there be enough room?
"Here's the pipe," Kyle coughed, "to make him look suave."
"And his scarf," Sondra said, "in the color of mauve."
And I had the last, the big black top hat;
A snowman's not done if he doesn't have that.
"Okay!" Now I told them, "I think that is all.
Everything's here to make our snowman real tall."

We all knew we could, despite what parents say,
A snowman we'd build on this hot summer's day,
We all gathered around, we were ready to go,
"Alright!" I exclaimed, "So who brought the snow?"

Note from C.M. Healy

Thank you so much for reading my collection of poems. If you liked *The Other Side,* with its rhymes and rhythm, you'll probably like the other children's books I have written. Once again, I appreciate you taking a chance on an unknown (for now) author.

Other children's books by C.M. Healy

The Lion and the Red Balloon & Other Silly Stories

If Mom Became an Octopus

Missing Numbers

I Can't

Penelope Rose

Preview the new young-adult novel by C.M. Healy

Beyond the After: Princess Lillian

Once the "I dos" were said, Snow White and Prince Charming did what every queen and king would do, start a family. They had a beautiful daughter, Princess Lillian, who has led a fairly uneventful life as far as princess' lives go. That is, until a faction of rogue Drodic citizens crashes her eighteenth birthday party, sending an ominous warning not only throughout the Valanti Kingdom, but also throughout the entire continent of Azshura. Now, a battle they thought was in their past has reemerged, threatening the lives of the people of Valanti, including its royal family—especially Lillian.

Can the mysterious figure who has entered her life be trusted?

As Lillian tries to discover who is targeting her, she must rely on the help of old friends and new, thus intertwining the lives of three famous queens and their eldest daughters in a way they couldn't have possibly imagined.

Lillian will have to push past boundaries she never knew existed as she is forced to choose between her responsibilities to her kingdom, or to the one she loves.

Preface

The battle of good and evil is a tale that's as old as the universe itself. Both have always existed, coexisted if you will, but they are not always equal. In truth, equality between the two is rarely the case. Evil does have its moments, but good has always seemed to have an upper-hand. Is it the edge of sacrifice versus selfishness? Loyalty opposed to treachery? Love over hate? What ever the mysterious power, more often than not good wins, in which case, peace is established for a period of time. It might be a year. It might be 100 years.

However, when one evil is vanquished another will arise attempting to shroud the land in darkness again, for that is the natural order of things. It is a delicate shift of momentum between these two, much like the swinging of a pendulum. One can never be sure what situation will spawn sinfulness nor what hardship will harbor heroics. And one can never be sure what the outcome will be. But one thing is for sure, it is during this fluctuation of powers in which the greatest stories ever told take place.

About the Author

C.M. Healy currently lives in Dallas, Texas with his wife, dog, and two giant cats where he taught seventh grade science. When he's not busy writing, he enjoys building Lego sets, playing video games, reading comic books (The Flash is his favorite), and watching TV with his best buddy, his wife. He earned the distinguished award of Eagle Scout during high school and went on to obtain his masters in child development from Oklahoma State University. He has been working with and entertaining children of all ages ever since.

amazon.com/authorcmhealy
authorcmhealy@gmail.com
Instagram & Twitter @authorcmhealy
cmhealy.tumblr.com

About the Illustrator

Emma Pate lives in Dallas, Texas, and is currently a student at Woodrow Wilson high school. She is passionate about all the arts, including theater, visual and musical arts. She loves to travel and hopes to explore and broaden her horizons as she does. She has had a wonderful experience illustrating and working with C.M. Healy on her first book and looks forward to similar opportunities in the future.

40016881R00025

Made in the USA
San Bernardino, CA
09 October 2016